The First Globals:

Understanding, Managing and Unleashing the Potential of Our Millennial Generation

John Zogby and Joan Snyder Kuhl

Copyright 2013

John Zogby and Joan Snyder Kuhl

# TABLE OF CONTENTS

Introduction ........................................................................................................................................3
    Who Are the First Globals?
    Why You Need This Book Right Now
    The Authors: Who We Are
    Why We Wrote This Book
    What You Will Find
    Who Should Read This

Part I: The First Globals: Eight Things You Need to Understand ..............................................11

Chapter 1: Globals and Their Multicultural World ....................................................................13

Chapter 2: Globals and the Changing Workplace ......................................................................15

Chapter 3: Globals and a Better World ........................................................................................23

Chapter 4: Globals and Horizontal Problem-Solving ................................................................29

Chapter 5: Globals and Mobility ...................................................................................................33

Chapter 6: Globals and Citizenship ..............................................................................................35

Chapter 7: Globals and Independence .........................................................................................41

Chapter 8: Impact of First Global Women ..................................................................................45

Part II: Management Strategies and Solutions to Unleash the Potential of First Globals .........49

Chapter 9: Harnessing the Talent and Effective Management Strategies ................................51
    For Senior Leaders
    For Managers
    For First Globals

Chapter 10: Scalable Global Training and Engagement Solutions to
    the Jobs Crisis and the Talent Gap ........................................................................................55

Chapter 11: A Presidential Summit Among Corporate and Wall Street Leaders… ..............59

Chapter 12: … And the Creation of America's First Globals Citizens Fund ..........................61

Chapter 13: First Globals Technology Corps ..............................................................................63

Conclusion .......................................................................................................................................65

Contact the Authors ........................................................................................................................67

Appendix: First Globals Demographics ......................................................................................70

# INTRODUCTION

## WHO ARE THE FIRST GLOBALS?

Let's begin by introducing The First Globals commonly referred to as Gen Y, the Millennials, or the Boomer Babies.

In my first book, *The Way We'll Be: The Zogby Report on the Transformation of the American Dream* (Random House, 2008), I wrote about four distinct age cohorts:

- **The Privates:** Born between 1926 and 1945, they are accomplished, and devoted to traditional values like duty, honor, patriotism, and family. They have paved the way in such trends as the civil rights movement and post-retirement encore living ("vol-work"), but they have done so quietly.

- **The Woodstockers:** The Baby Boomers, born between 1946 and 1964, are 78 million strong—a demographic phenomenon and a marketer's fantasy. A lot has been made of them at every stage of the life cycle, and they have internalized it all. The Woodstock Music Festival of 1969 was the ultimate testimonial to their self-indulgence, but they have raised children who share their values for a kinder, gentler world.

- **The Nikes:** Born from 1964 to 1978, they inherited a world that was falling apart. Just consider: assassinations, race riots, Vietnam, commodities shortages, Roe v. Wade, and a boomlet in divorces. They were forced to be on their own, to forge their own path, to just "Do It."

Enter the First Globals. For those Americans born between 1979 and 1994, history has invaded their sense of well-being and self, not once but twice. The signal event was, of course, the horror of September 11, 2001. If history were a guide, then predictably these high school and college students, along with their entry-level job colleagues, would have reacted by turning inward, rallying around the flag, wanting revenge—much like my older cousins and professors of the World War II era reacted to Pearl Harbor. But this group in their teens and twenties was already different. They played more soccer than baseball; they were the first to really watch and care about the World Cup. Technology from MTV to the Internet put them in touch with the rest of the world on a moment's notice. They wore and consumed global brands. And they were just starting to develop their own networks that included intimates or acquaintances who were not neighbors or in their gym class.

They were already, in other words, developing a global sensibility; geopolitical borders mattered less. Their world was already redefining space and geography. In 2005, Zogby International did a survey for an organization of major U.S. corporations called Business for Diplomatic Action. Their concern, following 9-11 and the U.S.-led war in Iraq was that both "American brands and the American brand" would suffer from international hostility. An interview with a very senior executive from the world's largest fast food chain shared that he was not terribly concerned because "we are not really seen as a U.S. company anyway." A poll on this question followed. The answer: American teens and twenty-somethings cared more about the product and less about where it was made or what nation it represented. They wore Louis Vuitton yet drank old-time (and very cheap!) Pabst Blue Ribbon. Their preferences weren't a matter of culture but of cool. In fact, *Advertising Age* underscored that finding with an article about how young Americans really didn't care anymore where a product came from—indeed, they were planetary "buyers without borders."

The tragedy of 9-11 made this group of young Americans even more curious about the rest of the world. Unlike their counterparts in China, Russia, and Brazil who have responded to a decade of enormous growth by searching for past imperial or divinely-inspired greatness, America's youth faced with tragedy came to the realization that perhaps the United States had reached the end of the road as the world's uni-power in both military and economic terms. All at once, they saw their country attacked and incapable of defeating the enemy; a collapse of the financial system; military interventions that split the nation and failed to achieve their goals; the intransigence of new and regional powers with their own global agendas; and a crisis in confidence in almost all of their familiar institutions following either their inability to provide solutions that required bipartisan solidarity or outright scandals that undermined trust. Iconic figures like Coach Joe Paterno, the local Catholic bishop, and the charismatic scout leader are just not the same any more.

Age cohorts are defined as much by significant historical events as they are by the life cycle. We know that "twenty-somethings" are always—how best to put it?—"twenty-something." They are generally focused more on the personal (career, relationship, looks, the now). But what makes any group fascinating is how history intrudes upon peoples' lives in the formative years and shapes the unique contribution that their "generation" makes to history. My mom and dad came of age during the Depression and, like the rest of their generation (to the point of cliché) they "knew the value of a dollar," unlike the spoiled children of the 1950s and '60s who wasted money as if there were no tomorrow.

Today's First Globals are a generation born and nurtured in crisis. Coddled at home, they have been given an extended lease on adolescence. But they have been witness to two cataclysms and have the training, desire, facility with new technologies, and the compassion to want to make their damaged world a better place. In recent Zogby Polls, as many as one in three prefer to be called "citizens of the planet Earth," more than any other age cohort.

## WHY YOU NEED THIS BOOK RIGHT NOW

We have such high hopes for our First Global generation. In a transformative era, they are the transformative agents. They are not steeped in or bound by old (obsolete) habits. They are ready to plunge in and make their world a better place. But they need to be understood, respected, and unleashed. This book has been developed to help readers get a better understanding of who the First Globals are and how best to integrate their skills into a world that really needs them.

## THE AUTHORS: WHO WE ARE

We are two distinct voices. A Baby Boomer ("Woodstocker") who has taught high school (four years) and college (20 years), who has been an employer for 26 years, and has polled and consulted on demographic changes for four decades. Above all, my wife and I have raised three sons born in 1978, 1980, and 1983.

And a First Global who has been in the workforce for 12 years leading multi-generational teams and those dominated by First Globals in the areas of sales, marketing, and training with successful results. She has spoken on high school and college campuses since 2000 and has built a network of First Global leaders from all over the world whom she mentors and coaches.

### John Zogby

Called "The Prince of Polling" and "the maverick predictor," John Zogby is the founder of the Zogby Poll, which assisted him in producing among the most accurate polling results for every U.S. presidential election since 1996. He has also distinguished himself in election polling in Canada, Mexico, Brazil, Venezuela, Dominican Republic, Israel, Lebanon, Palestine, Albania, and Iran.

Zogby is the former president and CEO of Zogby International and remains by all accounts the hottest pollster in the United States today. Since 1996, Zogby has polled for Reuters News Agency, the largest news agency in the world, and in 2000 polled for NBC News, the network news watched by most Americans. His media clients have also included MSNBC, the New York Post, Fox News, Knight-Ridder Newspapers, Gannett News Service, Houston Chronicle, Miami Herald, Atlanta Journal Constitution, the Albany Times Union, the Buffalo News, the St. Louis Post-Dispatch, the Cincinnati Post, the Cleveland Plain Dealer, the Toledo Blade, the Pittsburgh Post Gazette, the Rochester Democrat, and nearly every daily newspaper in New York State, as well as television stations throughout the United States.

He has polled, researched, and consulted for a wide spectrum of business, media, government, and non-governmental groups including Coca Cola, Microsoft, CISCO Systems, Philip Morris, St. Jude's Children's Research Hospital, MCI, Reuters America, UNAIDS, the World Health Organization, the Department of Defense, and the United States Census Bureau since 1984. Zogby continues to poll extensively throughout the world—at last count in more than 80 countries. He writes regular columns for Forbes, the Washington Examiner, and Credit Suisse's The Financialist.

### Joan Snyder Kuhl

After a decade of mentoring and leading thousands of First Globals from around the world to help them achieve their potential, Joan Snyder Kuhl launched Why Millennials Matter, a Gen-Y speaking and consulting company based in New York City. Why Millennials Matter is focused on raising awareness among employers about the value of investing in their future workforce.

While pursuing a career in the fields of business and health care, Joan has used her background of leadership in both the private and social sectors. Joan has more than 12 years of corporate management experience working at a Fortune 500 company in the roles of sales, marketing, organizational effectiveness, training, and development. She has been recognized for her turnaround tactics leading teams to high performance results and developing corporate-wide training and marketing initiatives.

The experience of coaching and mentoring First Globals about workforce issues—and being responsible for managing and developing them in a corporate environment— gives Joan a unique perspective.

## WHY WE WROTE THIS BOOK

### Zogby:

Back when young people used to like hearing stories from their elders, I recall my college professors and favorite older cousins recalling how they were just kids—hoping to catch a sight of some "knees," loving to see what sheer nylons did to the female leg, enjoying cheap wine (by the box, of course), and riding in fancy cars—until December 7, 1941. "The next morning," according to my economics professor James Kenney, "the lines were so long at the draft board, we were worried we wouldn't be able to enlist." That day, young boys and girls became the men and women of the Greatest Generation.

Already stunned by the horrible attack on the United States of September 11, 2001, America's First Globals were then socked in the jaw by an equally devastating blow—the recession beginning in 2008 which, at least to them, shows no sign of going away. An age cohort so facile in new and changing technologies, unwashed in the world of vertical/bureaucratic decision-making, in touch with global non-governmental organizations and passionate about resolving social problems, unphased by outmoded geographic and cultural borders, wanting to both change the world and go to work –but so many of them cannot get started. I have always been networked with other information companies and the world of not-for-profit organizations. I used to be able (and pleased) to offer fatherly advice and provide employer networking opportunities for college graduates—and those who simply wanted to take a break from their studies—and help them find a place to show off and really capitalize on their unique skills. If I didn't hire them myself, or place them in a great internship, I was usually able to find a place for them within a couple of degrees of my own network.

But as this Great Recession has lingered, I find myself relegated to giving them only personal advice. "Re-do your resume," I tell them. "Don't emphasize your college or advanced degree, everyone has one (or two) of those, along with a 3.6 grade point average. Tell me how you have used your own unique skills to solve a problem, find some missing money, bring warring colleagues together to reach consensus, been a group leader, even triumphed in a video game that required planning or cunning." I also tell them—in the typical fashion of a man d'un certain age—"I guess it's better to experience your financial crisis in your twenties than in your forties." But that is not enough. I am finding a small but growing sub-group within our First Globals who are victims of this long-term downturn, a group I call CENGAs—College-Educated Not Going Anywhere. And this is not just a series of personal tragedies. This could add up to a Lost Generation—of people who, on one hand, are so needed to move our communities and world to a new place, yet, on the other hand, simply cannot get started.

So my goal for writing about our First Globals is to showcase both their promise and potential, and the possible lost opportunity, if we do not act now.

### Kuhl:

In 2001, the mayor of Pittsburgh had a task force aimed at figuring out why such large numbers of the young people who attend the 33 colleges and universities in the area were leaving Pittsburgh after graduation. Pittsburgh ranks sixth in the nation for student concentration. At the time, I was student body president at the University of Pittsburgh, which had the largest student population (about 32,000) in the area, and so I was asked to participate in this initiative. The influence of my efforts sparked my passion for helping communities and organizations attract and retain young talent. Since then, I have coached and mentored thousands of First Globals to help them declare and define their career goals and make an impact in the workforce in every sector. My 12-plus years of corporate management experience, of hiring, developing, promoting, and sometimes firing Millennials, coupled with these first-hand experiences with the First Global generation shape my unique perspective for writing this book with John.

In 2009, I helped launch the Global Academy for Student Leadership based at The University of Pittsburgh in the name of my long time mentor, Frances Hesselbein. Frances is the former CEO of the Girls Scouts of the USA and was awarded the Presidential Medal of Freedom for her work as a pioneer for women, volunteerism, diversity, and opportunity by President Bill Clinton. Through mentoring relationships, social interaction, and instructional and interactive presentations, students in the Academy use critical thinking skills to address challenges offered by civic engagement sites throughout Pittsburgh and develop personal action plans to improve their community and/or campus.

My experiences and long-term relationships with the five annual cohorts of Academy students (each composed of 25 from all over the world representing countries such as Ghana, Pakistan, Finland, Australia, Sweden and 25 from across the United States) has taught me a great deal about their shared struggles in finding the right career fit that aligns with their values and goals to make a difference. As a mentor, it's important for me to convey the realities and expectations of today's workplace while encouraging them to become change makers and introduce new thinking and methods into traditional organizations. They need a blend of clear direction, structure, and motivation to empower them to find their place in the world.

As a corporate leader in the health care industry, my career has been shaped by the experiences of leading multi-generational teams through change, innovation, regulatory challenges, and organizational uncertainty. My affinity and passion for developing young professionals has given me insight into the right prescription to keep them engaged in an organization and help them grow into mature leaders with executive presence. Unfortunately, my optimistic vision for this generation is not widely shared or prioritized by my peers and senior leadership across all sectors. The dismissive attitude and lack of patience for Gen Y is a serious impediment to workplace productivity and the core reason why organizations are losing young talent. My motivation for writing this book is to represent the needs of both sides of the table, the organization and the talent. Think of me as the Millennial Matchmaker™, connecting the talent in the First Global generation to organizations and keeping them there for the long haul.

## WHAT YOU WILL FIND IN THIS BOOK

There will be a lot of polling data, but this is not a polling book. There will be profiles of First Globals who are changing the world and the workplace, including stories of their struggles and successes. It is an update on a group we have been writing, studying, and speaking about for years. It is a guide to the latest news about their lives and their world, a how-to book about why they are vital to our present and future, how to understand them and manage them, what they bring to the table that we cannot live without.

## WHO SHOULD READ THIS BOOK

- **Leaders** across all sectors who need to finally and decisively come to grips with what First Globals have to offer and consciously make room for them at the table.

- **First Globals** who need to be inspired, to be reminded that these hard times are a passing phase, that too many stereotypes about you are wrong. You will see how you actually fit into the broader context and how best to package yourselves. You should not have to wait 60 years like The Greatest Generation to find out who you are and what you mean in history.

- **Change makers, mentors and advocates for First Globals' success** who, like managers and employers, are on the frontline and need to make constant adjustments in order to advance change. This book offers a broader perspective and context about the meaning of this group and how best to manage and work with them.

- **Skeptics and those who are frustrated with Millennials** who need to recognize that the 72 million First Globals are the largest age cohort after Baby Boomers, and the world today needs them as much as the 1940s needed the "Greatest Generation." There are too many misconceptions and stereotypes that do not make our lives better or help our businesses become more productive and sustainable.

- **Parents of Millennials** who need to know that the period of "extended adolescence" or "adulthood deferred" will end. You have done everything you were supposed to do: You have nurtured your children to care about the larger world, paid to open up the larger world to them, provided them with a great education. You have much to be proud of. They will move out and beyond, but this process needs a sustained effort by the greater "village."

# PART I

# THE FIRST GLOBALS

## Eight Things You Need to Understand

# CHAPTER 1: GLOBALS AND THEIR MULTICULTURAL WORLD

Even while some of the optimism of this group has surely dampened with the lingering of the Great Recession, the First Globals strongly maintain their planetary sensibilities. In an April, 2013, Zogby Analytics poll, 35% said they are likely to "live and work in the capital of a foreign country" during their lifetime. While that number is down from 40% achieved right before the economy crashed, it is higher than the figure reported in *The Way We'll Be* in 2008 (23%), and substantially higher than any other age cohort.

| "How likely is it that you will live and/or work in a capital of a foreign country during your lifetime?" | | | | |
|---|---|---|---|---|
| | First Global | Nike | Woodstocker | Private |
| Likely | 35 | 23 | 12 | 2 |

More have traveled abroad than any other age cohort and more say they will have traveled to three or more continents in their lifetime—37%—substantially more than any other age group.

This group, almost the full beneficiary of integrated schools and advertising images, is much less likely than all other age cohorts, to agree that the cultures of Latin America, Asia, Africa, the Middle East, and elsewhere are inferior to American culture.

| Percentage who agree that American culture is superior to the culture of: | | | | |
|---|---|---|---|---|
| | First Global | Nike | Woodstocker | Private |
| China | 41 | 46 | 51 | 58 |
| S.E. Asia | 49 | 54 | 52 | 72 |
| Other Asia | 45 | 48 | 55 | 65 |
| Africa | 46 | 56 | 65 | 70 |
| Arab | 47 | 53 | 67 | 71 |
| Europe | 43 | 40 | 48 | 52 |
| Latin America | 48 | 55 | 62 | 66 |

They have not quite defined for themselves a color-blind world, but the movie of their lives is definitely in technicolor. First Globals are the most ethnically and racially diverse generation yet, and are also considered the most tolerant. Minorities make up 39% of this group, compared to just 27% of Baby Boomers and 20% of those born during the Great Depression and World War II.

Nearly two in five First Globals report that they have or have had a boss who is "of a different color" and a majority have either dated or would date a person of a different color.

Two in three (66%) have passports and have traveled abroad. But there is even more: The whole world is literally at their fingertips. Their frame of reference is so much larger than the world of other cohorts. I recall when my wife and I signed up our oldest son for the American Youth Soccer Organization in 1984. I volunteered to coach and at the start of our first practice, the father of one of the five year olds called me aside and said, "John, I am expecting that you will teach the kids the fundamentals of the game." Huh? I didn't know anything about soccer because we never played it. I played Little League and Babe Ruth Baseball and Catholic Youth Organization Basketball in the 1950s and '60s. As a pre-teen and teen, there was the occasional immigrant from Italy, Hungary, or Poland who would take out a soccer ball—but they never had anyone to play with them. Meanwhile, the world of our kids has been built around AYSO soccer, the World Cup, the adventures of Manchester United, Grammy and Academy Awards awarded to foreign actors and films, musicians from all over the world, Algerian Rai, Chinese Hip Hop, United Colors of Benetton, and immigrants in their communities from near and far.

By far and away, First Globals are more aware of the importance of the need to speak a foreign language.

| "How important is speaking a foreign language fluently to you?" | | | | |
|---|---|---|---|---|
|  | First Global | Nike | Woodstocker | Private |
| Very Important/ Somewhat Important | 60 | 46 | 27 | 29 |
| Very Important | 33 | 18 | 7 | 8 |

This is the first generation to have benefited from integrated schools, including a national percentage of college students that is around 15% minority. Their experience with diversity means that they will not need expensive "diversity training courses" and sensitivity training seminars. They themselves are the transition to the next America.

# CHAPTER 2: GLOBALS AND THE CHANGING WORKPLACE

In many ways First Globals have been coddled and made to feel special, but they have their own rules of engagement, which spill over into their work ethic and behavior. As noted in Chapter 1, having grown up with diversity in school and in their social networks, they are less in need of diversity training; however, cultural communication training or global market-specific training would be valuable to them. Most universities and colleges have expansive language programs which could better serve the First Globals as leaders of tomorrow by partnering with business schools to offer courses that address cultural business norms and communication differences with a geographic focus. These courses could serve as core curriculum or be offered not solely as prep for students planning to participate in study-abroad programs, but also for those seeking full-time positions with global corporations and entering a workforce of unique teams.

First Globals are also the most socially tolerant of all age groups. There is room for everyone in their world. While bullying still exists to a horrifying extent, it has become a major issue because it is so uncharacteristic of today's young people. Familiarity with social networks has placed them directly in touch with their own independent sources of news and problem solving. The children of "soccer moms," they have been scheduled to death—their parents' neurotic search for perfection resulted in tight schedules packed with Suzuki violin, tennis, lacrosse, playtime, and school. As a consequence, First Globals know how to work, how to show up on time, and how to produce. They work independently but their "big ideas" come from teams, from workplace "organized playtime."

## PROFILE

As Student Government president of Babson College in Wellesley, Massachusetts, **Rayshawn Whitford** stood out for his professionalism and passion for learning more about value-based leadership. His goals included working abroad after graduation and pursuing a career where he could use his creativity to inspire others and have a global impact.

Rayshawn was offered a tremendous opportunity post-graduation to become the Country-Director for Babson's Rwanda Entrepreneurship Center. His responsibilities included organizing Global Entrepreneurship Week (GEW) and preparing grant proposals for a teacher training program. In 2011, the week consisted of 26 events hosted by 22 partners and drew 12,000 participants. The goal for 2012 was 49 events hosted by 42 partners and double the participation of 2011.

Rayshawn shared his concerns about developing his competency and education in the Rwandan business and community culture:

"I'm worried that I haven't developed a deep enough understanding of the Rwandan culture. I think that my predecessors' lack of deep cultural understanding has hindered their progress over the last two years and I would like to build on what they've done and what they've learned by integrating ourselves into the business culture. The organization is looking to improve the entrepreneurial ecosystem here in Rwanda so that the country can continue its impressive economic growth through the next decade. Aside from hosting GEW/Rwanda we also host a seminar for secondary school students every summer that teaches them about the entrepreneurial mindset and gives them the confidence to take ownership of their ideas and to make them happen instead of looking for others to make their ideas happen. We're also hoping to begin a training program for entrepreneurship teachers in secondary schools to increase the impact our program and curriculum has throughout Rwanda.

"I've learned a lot of new things while I've been here and can't even begin to explain how valuable my experience has been when it comes to further developing my cross-cultural awareness. Rwanda couldn't be further from the U.S. when it comes to business culture so it's really forced me to keep a sharp eye on interactions and dealings here."

Rayshawn has grown his network beyond Rwanda to include leaders across East Africa and has spent time teaching in Uganda at Babson's Entrepreneurship Leadership Academy. The Root, an online newspaper published by The Slate Group (a division of the Washington Post Company), named Rayshawn to the 2013 Young Futurist List, an honor bestowed on the year's best and brightest black innovators ages 16 to 22.

### Growing Up Global

The First Globals grew up being given very specific instructions for every assignment in school and carefully laid out paths for getting into and succeeding in college. They have a tendency not to ask for details because they assume they already have them. As a result, they often fail to speak up in the workplace and ask for help or additional information. When First Global employees don't know what they don't know, it becomes critical that management facilitate an environment where all can be open to sharing the needed tacit knowledge.

These Millennial employees also tend to lack awareness of cultural business norms, contributing to friction with tenured peers and managers. For them, the business world does not have a distinct electric fence separating their personal mannerisms from their workplace behavior. They do not experience an identity shift when they walk into the workplace from the persona that defines their friendships and other personal relationships. This becomes a challenge in traditional environments where they have an uncontrolled need to express themselves, which may offend, turn off, or agitate older co-workers and managers.

There is still enough respect for "us" (i.e., silver-haired John Zogby Americans) to expect us to be their leaders and role models. Opportunity lies in the investment of tenured professionals to lead by example and make the effort to discuss expectations with First Globals, while being open to evolving workplace practices that suit "them."

It's time to debunk the stereotype that this generation is a bunch of slackers. It's easy to assume that someone is not as committed to working hard if they don't conform to a traditional 9-5 work week and request days off within three months of hire. However, the First Global generation is the first to be immersed in the 24/7 world of business. Smart devices and wireless Internet have extended the workday far beyond the hours when you are physically in the office. Older professionals (boomers and veterans) are more aligned to the 9-5 mentality or the "you work 'til the work is done" attitude. Baby boomer or veteran professionals are not the employees requesting to work from home or to call-in remotely for meetings.

Despite the negative label of laziness, First Globals work just as many hours as the Baby Boomers did at this stage in the '70s. As mentioned earlier, they are the first generation to be employed in 24/7 non-stop environments. They are putting in just as much time at this stage, but not in the traditional 9-5 structure. Management needs to try and understand First Globals' style to determine common ground about expectations for work completion and participation, with some compromise to their comfort level.

Additional friction with management can arise because of the distinct approach of First Globals to career advancement. Historically, such advancement was built upon seniority and time of service, but First Globals want to progress much more quickly. When older employees view advancement in the traditional sense, they can be skeptical of First Globals' pursuit of a fast-track rise to the top, particularly when these younger co-workers clearly have no second thoughts about seizing opportunities and leap-frogging over more senior colleagues. First Globals value results over tenure and are sometimes frustrated with the amount of time it takes to climb the career ladder. Globals have to be more respectful of the traditional mindset, but diplomatically address their priority on results. With tact and grace, Globals need to highlight their successes without bragging or failing into self-aggrandizement.

Eighty-five percent of First Globals—again higher than any other age cohort—say that achieving a "useful and beneficial life experience" from their workplace is very or somewhat important. They want learning opportunities and projects that can build their skill base. They want to work with friends, people they click with (both socially and literally). They want our respect, they want to be flexible—after all they need a break from "karate at 4PM, tennis at 6:20PM, and piano virtuosity from 9PM-9:20PM." We need to create office space so they are physically in a place where they can share ideas. And they want to be "reverse mentors"—they have a lot to teach their older colleagues and managers about technology, e-commerce, and groupthink.

## PROFILE

In 2008, **Laryssa Wozniak** was a young analyst at a mid-size pharmaceutical company with aspirations to join a pre-launch product In 2008, Laryssa Wozniak was a young analyst at a mid-size pharmaceutical company with aspirations to join a pre-launch product team. After several years of successful reviews and responsibilities that mainly centered on analytics and market research, she made the decision to pursue her MBA full-time with concentrations in Marketing and Pharmaceutical Management.

This talented and driven young woman was interested in living abroad and gaining insight about the global market to further her impact as a leader one day for a product or brand team. At the same time that Laryssa earned acceptance to Rutgers University in New Brunswick, NJ, she was offered a lateral career opportunity within her current company to join a successful product brand team and handle sales promotion activities in the United States. Laryssa gracefully made the decision to go back to school and expand her expertise. She graduated at the top of her class at Rutgers through the Pharmaceutical Management MBA program and had several highly visible and competitive internships which led to multiple job offers from pharmaceutical and bio-technology companies. She chose to accept an offer from GlaxoSmithKline as a marketing manager in their Commercial Esprit Programme, a global leadership development initiative. For the next three years, Laryssa would serve in multiple roles of responsibility spanning several functions of the business.

Ultimately, Laryssa made the choice to invest in her own development, staying committed to her belief that educating herself about global business issues would best position her for success in her long-term career versus accepting a U.S.-based internal promotion.

First Globals know that many of their workplace experiences are going to be ephemeral. While 24% of all adults say it is likely that their career will be a series of "gig jobs vs. a long term job," that represents 32% of Globals (25% of Nikes and 22% of Woodstockers). The key that organizations misunderstand about this preference is that it does not need to be limited to company jumping. The gig job experience can be satisfied through global or cross-functional team rotations within the same company. First Globals will seek out the companies that offer them both challenging and stretch assignments especially if they require them to experience a new culture.

But there is an enormous roadblock that stands in the way of activating a more engaging and productive workplace for First Globals: So many of them are either out of work or underemployed. In April, 2012, it was reported that one in two new college graduates in the United States were either unemployed or underemployed. Underemployment is defined as either working part-time but looking for full-time employment (e.g., someone picking up shifts at a restaurant or in retail while pursuing employment that aligns with the education they spent a small fortune on)—or holding a position that doesn't fully maximize the skills, knowledge, or training of the employee. Having taken a job for a paycheck, it's likely that an underemployed Global will have productivity below expectations—and one foot out the door looking for a better opportunity.

The culture of dis-engagement and poor results will compound unless this group is directed toward roles that better align with their skills. First Globals struggle with maintaining realistic expectations for entry-level jobs. This leads to conflict with management and older generations from the outset.

But they want more than just a job—they want a life-changing experience for themselves, for their fellow workers, and for the people that they serve. Their expectations are very high. In a 2006 survey by CONE, Inc., 79% of Millennials said they "want to work for employers who care about how they impact/contribute to society" and 44% said they would "actively pursue working for a company after they learned about their company's commitment to social issues." In a July, 2012, Zogby Poll, we learned that Americans born between 1979 and 1994 are the most likely to say it is "very or most important to have the opportunity to do something that changes the world" (71%). They are pretty much tied with those born between 1964 and 1978 (70%) but substantially outnumber Boomers (62%) and Privates (51%).

Again, First Globals were taught by their parents to care about others. Being overloaded by debt and worry only increases the tension between finding a job and doing some good.

## PROFILE

**Luke Owings** is currently the Head Coach at the Fullbridge Program with the responsibility of playing coach to the coaches. Based in Harvard Square (Cambridge, MA), the Fullbridge Program is a four-week intensive and transformative curriculum that prepares highly motivated undergraduates and recent graduates from all fields of study for a successful transition to the working world. It's the ideal boot camp for First Global graduates who are committed to developing core qualities that will help them excel and navigate their career across all sectors. (We will share more about the Fullbridge Program and other scalable training models in Part 2 of this book.)

As Head Coach, Luke recruits passionate professionals with credible experience and an appreciation for the difference they can make in a student's life. Luke's path to Fullbridge began as an athlete and community leader during his undergraduate years at Princeton, followed by two years working for McKinsey & Co. at locations around the world. After McKinsey, Luke was accepted into Harvard Business School, where he also taught Intro to Economics to Harvard undergraduates. His story and path align well with our thoughts on growing up global and the changing workplace. Luke traveled around the world during college with his older brother and as an associate with McKinsey, which sparked his desire to pursue work that would impact young people around the globe.

*On education:* "Teaching was really a game-changer for me because it was the fulfillment of so many of the things that I had loved so far in my life. Mostly, it allowed me to focus on creating an environment that brings out the best in people and allows them to transform themselves. While at McKinsey, I had learned the value of an on-the-ground manager who would mentor me and teach me how to be effective. It's there that my career path as a developer of young people started to take shape. What my first manager did for me made me ready, once I was at Harvard Business School, to take on the mantle of teaching young people at the college. During my time at HBS, I became a Teaching Fellow and, at that point, it was clear how much value I received and could create by helping young people gain clarity, confidence, and peace while they're transitioning at inflection points in their lives. Fortunately, this vision I was building for my life was in line with the vision of the company that one of my favorite HBS professors was starting to build. After one visit, I was sold on the idea of joining Peter Olson (former Chairman and CEO of Random House) and Candice Carpenter Olson (former founder and CEO of iVilliage) at Fullbridge and helping them change the education landscape."

*On his career goals:* "My career goals for the future are to bring the best the world has to offer into the educational sphere and shape the educational landscape by running a mission-based organization that seeks to empower a group of people by giving them access to an environment where they can learn, grow, and become their best self. Most of all, I want Fulbridge to build an ecosystem with which people from all walks of life can find value and create new things. In doing that, I want to become a place that attracts, develops, and retains those with an open mindset that believes, to the core of their being, that life is not zero-sum.

"My work environment is definitely a core driver of my productivity and satisfaction. Being a part of a mission-driven organization with people who believe in our vision is crucial to being able to devote my whole self to the goals. Further, it becomes very tempting to get caught in a competition with my peers from both McKinsey and HBS as we all take on higher and higher roles with more and more pay. Being in an environment that I believe in makes those external measures matter a whole lot less in terms of my satisfaction and allows me to be at peace with the NOW."

*On Millennials at work:* "Millennials that I've worked with have a tremendous capability for collaborative creation. Throughout their lives, they've gained more and more access to tools of production as well as an understanding that the world is an open place. Hence, when put into a situation where they feel part of something, they're amazingly creative and non-provincial. There's an understanding with them that new things can be created and they're not going to be created unilaterally.

"I hardly think that this generation is not willing to work hard. In fact, for many, the line between work and home has been blurred to the point where they're willing to work all the time if given the opportunity to do so in a way that they value. That said, I think that this generation is more dependent on having someone structure their environment and to motivate them. Call it a product of the amalgamation of the video-game era and the overscheduled childhood, it's not always natural for them to be proactive shapers of their experience. Given that, there's a need to transform mindsets into ensuring that they recognize they are the driving force behind who they become.

"Finally, I do think that this generation is so used to having an abundance of opportunities in an environment with low switching costs that they're willing to jump around a bit too much. This happens because they either don't like the discomfort of really building something or because they want to 'hack life' to get to the top. From my perspective, both of these are a constant temptation (and not bad in and of themselves) so need to be consciously recognized throughout early careers."

# CHAPTER 3: GLOBALS AND A BETTER WORLD

First Globals are civic-minded and are revolutionizing the world of NGOs. While Spring Break is still likely to bring them to the beaches of southern California and south Florida, a small but growing number fly to the Cameroons, Haiti, and other needy destinations to do volunteer work. The increase in applications for programs like Teach for America and the Peace Corps are evidence of this altruistic orientation. These volunteer experiences and the media spotlight on mission-focused leaders such as Blake Mycosie of Tom's Shoes; the founders of Warby Parker; Liz Forkin Bohannon, founder of Sseko Designs; Simon Sinek; Seth Godi; Jessica Alba who launched The Honest Company; Wendy Kopp of Teach for America; Lincoln Brown, co-founder of SoJo Studios; and Rashmi Sinha, founder of SlideShare, have inspired First Globals to focus on social business models and launch entrepreneurial ventures that aim to solve a global or local issue.

They are the children of the children of the '60s and share a lot of their parents' values, one of which is to serve their community. "To Serve Is To Live" is the motto memorialized by Frances Hesselbein, 97, former CEO of Girls Scouts USA and current CEO of The Frances Hesselbein Leadership Institute. Ms. Hesselbein has traveled to more than 65 countries sharing her values-based leadership philosophy. "I spend one third of my time with new generation leaders, who give me renewed hope and energy. Their story is one that provides other young leaders inspiration and encouragement and we are grateful for the privilege of telling it," said Hesselbein. Her message to students all over the world through her campus tours and global webinar series sparks a universal reaction with First Globals who want to make a difference in their community.

But their "community" happens to be worldwide. In July, 2012, when a Zogby Analytics poll asked 1,129 adults nationwide how important it is for their workplace to provide an "opportunity to do something that changes the world," 71% of Globals replied it was very or somewhat important, more than any other age cohort. They are actively seeking companies who prominently share their corporate social responsibility priorities and community impact with an emphasis on strong values. Organizations that recognize volunteer work days as developmental opportunities without vacation penalty are magnets for First Globals.

Warren Buffet, Chairman and CEO of Berkshire Hathaway Inc., was recently interviewed by the Founder of Levo League, which defines itself as a "social good startup designed to elevate young women in the workforce by providing the career resources needed to achieve personal and professional success." He spoke to the entire First Global generation of men and women describing the attributes he feels are aligned with success and encouraging young people to seek out their passion. "You are lucky in life if you can find your passion. You may have to take a job or two because you've got to eat! But never give up searching for the job that is your passion. Find the job you would have if you were independently rich. When you find that job that causes you to be excited every day ... with people you love, doing what you love, it doesn't get any better than that."

An April, 2013, Zogby Analytics poll showed that almost two in three First Globals say it is important for them to contribute time and money to an international charity. As the following table reveals, their identification with global philanthropy is considerably greater than any other age cohort.

| "How important is it to you to contribute your time and money to an international charity?" | | | | |
|---|---|---|---|---|
| | First Global | Nike | Woodstocker | Private |
| Very Important/ Somewhat Important | 62 | 48 | 32 | 24 |

## PROFILE

Interview with **Julie Eckhart** and **Jeff Kurtzman,** co-founders of Operation Incubation (http://operationincubation.org). Julie's story exhibits the community-minded traits of the First Globals and Jeff's story exemplifies the desire for graduates to find work that makes a visible community difference beyond just the bottom-line.

*Julie:* "Ever since I was younger, I have had an inner desire to serve my community in a way that aligned with my own personal interest. Throughout middle school and high school I volunteered at a horse rescue farm, and also with the youth group at my local church. My best friend often organized PB&J parties at her house where we'd spend the night eating pizza and making literally hundreds of peanut butter and jelly sandwiches to deliver to homeless shelters in Baltimore.

"When I graduated from UVA [University of Virginia], I had a burning desire to really do something with my life and make a difference as a young person. I decided to take giving back to the next level and signed up to go on a medical mission trip to Port Maria, Jamaica. I served as a dental assistant, despite knowing little to nothing about medical care, and my eyes were opened to a new world of service; service at the most granular level, meeting individuals with the bare bones of what they needed most, just after food and water—medical care.

"During our trip debrief, I learned that the medical center our mission partnered with was in need of an incubator. The infant incubator a nonprofit had donated was broken, and there was no mechanic on the island to fix it, certainly not one that the medical center could afford with its concrete and dirt floors, sheet-less beds, and minimal equipment.

"There, something struck a chord in my heart and I felt very strongly that infant incubators should be something that every new mother and newborn should have access to. I had just moved to Washington, DC, for my first job, where it seemed there was a fundraiser for a new cause every night. Upon returning home, I solicited the help of my family friend, and seasoned social venture founder, Jeff Kurtzman, and we decided to launch a nonprofit that would focus on delivering sustainable infant incubators specifically designed for the developing world, to places like Port Maria, Jamaica.

"Jeff and I both work part-time, so it has been a definite challenge to get our nonprofit off the ground, but to date, we have sent seven incubators to Jamaica, Haiti, and Uganda and are working on a project in Somalia. We also launched a brand new website to help in our marketing and fundraising efforts. I can't wait to see what is next for our little nonprofit, and it feels good knowing that we have helped even one mom and baby."

[Julie is currently a digital journalist/associate producer in the DC bureau of NowThis News, a video news network start-up reinventing news on mobile, social, and online platforms for the Millennial generation. She recently graduated with a master's in journalism from Georgetown University.]

*Jeff:* "I grew up between Baltimore and DC in Maryland. I graduated from the University of Notre Dame in 2001 with a degree in Finance and Business Economics. After 18 months of non-stop work as an investment banking analyst at Deutsche Bank, I left to start up, along with two former college roommates, a social venture called Better World Books. Almost nine years later, our online bookstore has grown to over 300 employees and nearly $50 million in annual sales–but more importantly, we have donated nearly $10 million to non-profit literacy causes around the world, sent hundreds of thousands of books to where they are needed most, and saved nearly

60 million books from landfills. Since leaving my full-time role as CFO three years ago, I have been consultant for numerous startups and am currently helping out a 'green' technology venture capital firm.

"For me, Operation Incubation started when Julie (my sister's best friend and my friend since she was born) e-mailed me after coming home from a medical mission to a very poor area of Jamaica. She said something like 'Hey Jeff! I have an idea…and I think you can help me get it off the ground…I'm calling it Operation Incubation.' She then told me all about her medical mission trip to Jamaica. While I had experience starting a for-profit social venture, I had never started a non-profit, but figured it would be an exciting challenge that, if successful, would make a huge impact! I figured, if we don't do this, who will?

"The next day I did some googling and was amazed to find out how big of a problem this really was…and how little was being done about it. I was blown away when I read that over 400 babies die every hour around the world (5+ million babies per year) due to the lack of incubators! Truly an unbelievably daunting figure! So many babies are not given a chance because a fairly simple piece of equipment is not available. What seemed like a fairly simply project…host some fundraisers in DC to send a few incubators to hospitals in Jamaica…was now, in my mind, becoming something much bigger.

"When we read that a very innovative non-profit called Embrace Global had recently designed and were piloting an incubator specifically for the developing world that could be produced for around $25 (versus $10,000-$20,000 for a hospital grade incubator), we quickly realized that with the help of donors and volunteers Operation Incubation could really make a huge difference…and help save many lives!

"Next, I checked in on one of my favorite charities, a cutting edge non-profit called Nothing But Nets, who have raised over $25 million to purchase bed nets that fend off malaria-carrying mosquitos in the developing world. Their non-profit had a mission much like ours, raise a relatively small sum of money to purchase a very simple device that could save life after life after life. The issue we identified (a high infant mortality rate) was very similar to malaria–it was a solvable problem! Julie and I have made it our goal to make just as big of an impact as Nothing But Nets."

I (Zogby) have had the opportunity to strategize for UNAIDS and the World Health Organization and have told them to begin to tap into First Globals, as an incredible source of energy and wealth. When the powerful earthquake rocked Haiti a few years ago, half a billion dollars was raised in 96 hours by texting donations of $10 and $20. Believe me, it wasn't me or my generational cohorts because we didn't know how to do that back in 2009.

When a special task force was formed by WHO in 2008 to discuss how best to reach their donor base, a meeting was convened in Geneva that I participated in by telephone. Also included via conference call were officials representing a major London-based public relations firm who were pushing for full –page newspaper ads in the London Times, the New York Times, and the Washington Post to appeal to major influencers among the readership base. I was able to remind them how much the rules of giving had changed, how technology made it easier to offer more intimate messaging to a far greater potential audience, and how then-Senator Barack Obama was able to raise huge amounts of money by going beyond the well-heeled major givers and by making direct appeals to millions of small donors. "What a powerful opportunity we have," I told the group, "to link front-line health care providers directly to potential givers via social media." I reminded them that nurses and physicians could now tweet short messages telling stories about children receiving medications, having their lives improved and even extended. Above all, this could be done on a person-to-person basis and to an entire new audience who wanted to help—just as they had helped so dramatically in Haiti.

# CHAPTER 4: GLOBALS AND HORIZONTAL PROBLEM-SOLVING

First Globals want to be engaged and want to build a better world; they are truly Global Citizens. And mobile and social media make that all possible.

This group of children has grown up in a world of 24-hour news (even when there isn't much news!), and immediate information is available to them in seconds. There is little mystery left when you are a twenty-something. This involves the trivial: Is Don Knotts alive or dead? Just how many thirty-something British actresses named Kate are there? Is it faster to turn right at the fork in the road or bear left? But it certainly involves things that are much more vital to their lives as well. Answers to these (and slightly more pressing problems and curiosities) are at our fingertips. There is little patience for resolving burgeoning crises. In our world, if a story is broken on CNN at noon, then it is a full-blown crisis by 5 PM if it has not yet been resolved.

Global Citizens respond to these situations—large and small—so differently than the ways we are accustomed to. Gone is the afternoon "emergency" meeting. This is why Millennials express frustration in the workplace when problems are drawn out to higher levels without progress on proposed solutions within an expedited time frame. Bureaucracy drives them crazy. Gone are the "task forces" to come back with "actionable items" in 48 hours. Gone is the "delegation" to take the problem one step up the chain—then further up until it dies and goes away. Our Global Citizens have lived in a world where major crises are averted within 53 minutes—the length of a network television drama, excluding commercial breaks. Their mandate and modus operandi is to find solutions in a hurry and to bypass vertical channels.

What makes this group so refreshingly different is that they eschew bureaucracy and seek solutions using social networks via crowdsourcing—posing the question to their network and waiting for immediate replies. Somewhere out there is a solution, it can be presented in short order, and further responses can be used to build on a core idea or for validation. This strategy allows this cohort to widen their pool of team players and not to fall victim to bureaucracies, which are more and more equipped to sustain ungainly structures and job descriptions, and less and less equipped to resolve problems.

This drills to the core of miscommunication and weak relationships with managers and First Globals' misalignment with corporate norms. This generation has a limited capacity for tolerating the slow churning approach to resolving problems that impact customers and efficiencies which will ultimately drive them out the door. In spite of their world, their nation, their city, their schools, and the non-profit organizations all around them being dominated by bureaucratic structures that are slow, cumbersome, and even dysfunctional, there are newer models that exist and can both enable and benefit from the special skills that First Globals bring to the table.

Public intellectual and author Parag Khanna describes a "next renaissance," a rejection of current practices of global problem-solving that lead to either entropy or to dysfunction. In his analysis, he compares the current epoch to the decline of feudalism and to the Renaissance-Protestant Reformation-Enlightenment where new structures arose to replace outmoded institutions. Today, he says, problem-solving must be transnational and involve much more than governments. His fixes include alliances of cities, civic groups, religious charities, corporations, "Super-NGOs," and celebrities. Just like the world of the First Globals, these actors are beyond borders, nimble, speedy, and broadly participatory. There is plenty of room for "independent diplomats" to be heard and to be involved.

A small cadre of young people based in New York has formed a network called AVAAZ that reaches 22 million activists (and growing) in 15 languages and on five continents. The AVAAZ network launches worldwide petition drives on a myriad of issues like anti-gay laws in Uganda, the treatment and near-extinction of elephants, the legal rape of young women in countries like India and Somalia, and the still-extensive use of pesticides. AVAAZ could not have existed even 10 years ago. Today petitions are circulated in moments and as many as one million signatures can be submitted on an issue. Sadly, not every issue means a victory—but some have won and millions are involved in democratic, horizontal movements for change.

## PROFILE

**Rachael Chong** is the founder and CEO of **Catchafire,** an organization that matches professionals who want to donate their time and skills with nonprofits and social enterprises that need their help. Catchafire is trying to create a more effective and efficient social good sector and a world where it is commonplace to serve. The mission is to provide talented individuals with transformational pro bono experiences in order to build capacity for social good organizations.

Rachael was a successful young investment banker looking to give back to her community in a meaningful way. One day, her firm offered a volunteer opportunity to help build a house in the Bronx. As Rachael's 5'2" frame slowly hauled lumber across the schoolyard, she realized that she wasn't volunteering in the most effective way. So, she spent the next six months looking for a better way to volunteer her time. Rachael was shocked at the lack of opportunities to volunteer her hard-earned skills and expertise. Frustrated by her inability to serve the greater good while keeping her day job, Rachael left corporate finance to work in microfinance. A year later, Rachael helped start-up BRAC USA, the U.S. affiliate of BRAC, one of the largest nonprofit organizations in the world. To accomplish this daunting task with limited staff and budget, Rachael had to think of inventive ways to use her resources. She turned to her network of friends and former colleagues, getting each to volunteer their time and expertise on short-term, discrete, and individual projects. By doing this, Rachael helped to free up the time of BRAC USA's full-time staff to raise millions of dollars in the organization's first year.

Fresh off her success with BRAC USA, Rachael founded Catchafire with the goal of making it easy for every professional to give their skills (without having to quit their well-paying jobs) and to make it easy for every nonprofit and social enterprise to leverage the goodwill of professionals. To date, Catchafire's pro bono professionals have given more than 45,000 valuable pro bono hours, resulting in $11 million in savings for their partner nonprofits and social enterprises. And that's just the direct savings. The multiplier effect of the relationships formed, expertise given, portfolios bolstered, and impact created go much further.

"I worked in finance for a few years at the beginning of my career, and I was disappointed by the lack of opportunities to use my professional skills to give back. I did a fair amount of traditional volunteering — I worked in soup kitchens, I stuffed envelopes, and while I think those opportunities are very important, I wanted something that would really leverage the skills I was building at my job. The more skilled professionals I spoke to about this, the more I found it was a pretty common sentiment. Then I read that more than 80% of young professionals want their career to address social good in some way. I found it astounding that it wasn't easier to find outlets for all that skill and good intention, because clearly there are many cash-strapped nonprofits in great need of professional services. So I founded Catchafire in hopes of making it easier to find that outlet. And the name is from one of my favorite Bob Marley songs.

"For the social good organizations we serve, it opens up a whole world of access to services they could never afford ordinarily or know where to find. Organizations can spend a lot of time and resources trying to figure out how to do something themselves when they don't have the staffing or money for it. When you bring in a pro bono professional, you're guaranteeing that the job will be done efficiently, and it frees up the organization's time and resources to devote to other important tasks. It's also great for the professional. We've heard many times that people who give pro bono through Catchafire have really benefited from the contacts they've made, and from working in a new setting. It can be great project-management experience, especially for early-career professionals or those hoping to switch career tracks. Pro bono looks great on a resume. And of course, giving back to a cause you really care about feels great, too!"

# CHAPTER 5: GLOBALS AND MOBILITY

This group wants to move around. They cannot be wedded to one place and one job because that world no longer exists. These Globals are our first inductees into the "Gig Economy." According to Princeton's Alan Blinder, today's twenty-somethings will have had four gigs by the age of 30, 10 by the age of 40. At the very least, this is a group not prepared to sink roots into one community and live out their lives and careers in a single place. We suggest that organizations can tackle this by providing accelerated development tracks, cross-functional and global rotations, or through multiple apprenticeships across core business operations. With these types of strategies not yet the norm at most organizations, the gig addiction can have a potentially positive impact on businesses rather than a negative one.

The Gig Economy can have serious implications for homeownership, perhaps a model of an America gone by. While a sense of "community" may not necessarily be defined by temporal space, it can still be alive in the hearts and minds of those who grew up in a town, lived there for a while, and hold a special place in their hearts for its people and well-being. That doesn't require paying school taxes, making United Way donations, or sending children to its public schools.

Globals have bought into the need to be mobile: 32% say they plan "stay at their current job three years or less." This may not seem like a high number, especially for an age group in the life-cycle that has been ready to sew its wild oats for years ("How ya gonna keep them down on the farm after they've seen Pa?"), but compare that 32% with only 25% of Nikes (1964-1978) who said the same thing. Their bags are packed and they are ready to move on and this has serious consequences for how we define housing, relationships, and children, connections to community, and skills-building for an eclectic series of gigs. Globals are less in the market for long-term housing and their living space will focus on "work" and "play," rather than on family, meals, or sociability.

| "As you look into the future, is your preference to plant roots in a community and settle down or would you prefer to be mobile in your life?" ||||| 
|---|---|---|---|---|
|  | First Global | Nike | Woodstocker | Private |
| Plant roots and settle down | 46 | 62 | 68 | 83 |
| Be mobile | 20 | 21 | 14 | 7 |
| Not sure | 34 | 17 | 18 | 8 |

The figures above are pretty clear, especially the numbers of First Globals who are just not sure what the future holds. No doubt, some of that is the uncertainty that is part of being "twenty-something." Some, to be sure, is the "Wanderlust" that also characterizes a generation where the whole world is now the playing field. But to "prefer to be mobile in your life" is an option that is certainly being considered.

# CHAPTER 6: GLOBALS AND CITIZENSHIP

Despite numerous warnings from political consultants and the pundit class, voters under 30 matched (and very possibly exceeded) their 2008 record turnout in the 2012 presidential election. There was no "enthusiasm gap" among young voters as had been predicted. In both elections, 18-29 year olds were about 19% of the total. In the 2004 election, they were only 17% of the total, which had been the norm. And, while Barack Obama did not receive the level of support among this group in 2012 as had thrust him into the White House in 2008 (66%), he did get 61% against Republican nominee former Massachusetts Governor Mitt Romney. Thus, while Senator John Kerry defeated President George W. Bush among young voters by 9 percentage points in 2004, President Obama has defeated his GOP opponents by 32 points in 2008 and 25 points in 2012. While Mr. Obama's victories were by substantial margins, his support among young voters clearly put him over the top.

Half of First Globals are voting. That in itself is a record for twenty-somethings.

First Globals do not distrust government, however they are wary of politicians. According to John Della Volpe, the director of polling at Harvard's Institute of Politics, among the reasons that 50% of First Globals are not voting is a lack of trust in politicians—which has spiked downward as a result of the recession of 2008—and Washington's failure to include them in political discussions, especially those related to their financial future.

But, at least for now, Democrats benefit from the two dominant strains among this age cohort. On the one hand, there are the problem-solvers who want action on problems and do not want to dither and ignore issues like disparity in incomes, America's image overseas, global warming, and human rights. On the other hand, there are libertarian free-spirits in the full sense of the term: They fear intrusion in their private lives. They are disgusted with debt—both their own and that of the federal and state governments. And they certainly do not want anyone peering into their bedrooms, on their websites, or overseeing their social media habits. Democrats have a default advantage here.

First Globals are also a group that is aware and engaged. As I (John) have told audiences for years, "They may not know exactly where Darfur is one the map, they certainly know that there is a Darfur," and this makes them stand out among other age cohorts. The Charles F. Kettering

Foundation has been studying the values and priorities of college students since 1993. They have found a growing level of engagement among the current First Globals who are now in their twenties and thirties. From 1993 to 2006, their surveys have shown a greater degree of experience in volunteerism and increased belief in "their obligation to work together with others on social issues." Today's First Globals are also, according to the Dayton, Ohio-based foundation researchers, more involved locally with others, "more comfortable and experienced with direct service and turned off by politics."

This is a group who overall dislike spin and prolonged debates, according to the Kettering study, and they "seek authentic opportunities for discussing public issues." First Globals also dislike the "competitive atmosphere of parties … [thus they seek out] reliable information so that they can critically develop their own opinions." The 2006 study applauded this age cohort for developing "calm opinions and the authentic sharing of ideas."

Other studies reinforce the fact that First Globals are notably good citizens. A June 2007 survey by progressives Peter Leyden and Ruy Texeira projects that by 2016, one in three citizen-eligible voters and 30% of all actual voters will be First Globals—a percentage, they suggest, that may even grow as they proceed through the life cycle. Leyden and Texeira argue that this age cohort has been voting heavily Democrat since the 2006 elections; in 2013, in our own Zogby Polls, 48% identify as Democrats. Whether this changes or not, and only time and events will tell, this group is interested and very involved.

And they support change to the status quo. On April 17, 2013, a Fox News intern Karen Hackett published an article entitled, "Creating Their Own Change: Millennials Pair Politics With Volunteer Work." Hackett refers to several organizations of, by, and for First Globals that promote social change.

For example, *Generation Opportunity* is a national, non-partisan effort whose founder Evan Feinberg explains: "Young people are disillusioned with the idea that hope and change can come from Washington. They are ready for the government to get out of the way so that they can drive real change." Feinberg says that Millennials are more focused on local communities where they can "create their own change" because they "don't trust politicians."

Ms. Hackett also cites the formation of *Mobilize.org,* which "empowers young people to create and implement their own solutions to social issues."

Finally, *Our Time* is an organization that, according to its co-founder Matthew Siegel, "wants a government that is efficient and politicians that are long-term-oriented in investment and sensibility."

### Globals and Hopes Deferred

But there is reason to be worried about a growing subset of First Globals—the CENGAs, i.e. college educated and not going anywhere. This nearly four-year recession and general slowdown has taken its toll. I remember well the twenty-somethings who used to visit or write me looking not for a job at my company but for the quickest path to becoming chief operating officer. Gone is a lot of that cockiness and it isn't simply that I miss it; I am thinking about all of the wasted human capital. These kids are well trained, enthusiastic, quick to solve problems, and eager to network with fellow Globals worldwide. They bring so much to the table: They are not steeped in my cohort's formula for solving problems big and small (i.e., move it up the ladder and at some point it will just go away). They use their networks, grow them, nurture them, and believe in them. And they have made a believer out of me. But for now, their skills and their enthusiasm languish.

Paul Mason of *The Guardian* has been musing about the Arab Spring ("From Arab Spring to Global Revolution," February 5, 2013; "Twenty Reasons Why It's Kicking Off Everywhere," February, 2011), but his commentaries chillingly describe the plight of twenty-somethings worldwide, including the West.

> … [T]here [is] a new sociological type at the heart of the global protests: the graduate with no future. … Without some massive and cathartic turnaround, the generation in their 20s, in the West, will never accumulate pay, conditions or savings at the level their parents did. What they are accumulating is resentment… [This is] the rise of the networked individual colliding with the economic crisis.

Now, we don't sense there will be a massive revolt in the United States. But we do see wasted opportunity. The best and brightest of our nation, those with so much desire and capability, the ones we need the most to infuse new thinking and new approaches to resolving problems turning inward, are becoming filled with resentment, draining their energies in a battle to stay solvent to be relevant.

Our colleagues at Harris Interactive conducted their annual poll on stress in early 2013 and the results were reported in *USA Today* ("Who's Feeling Stressed? Young Adults, New Survey Shows," February 7, 2013).

| "On a scale of 1 to 10, with 1 being 'little or no stress' and 10 being 'a great deal of stress'" ||
|---|---|
| All groups | Average  4.9 |
| 18-33 year olds | Average 5.4 |

First Globals (those between the ages 18 and 33) were the only age cohort who reported that their stress had increased in the past year. Two in five (39%) said that it had increased. A majority (52%) said that their stress had kept them awake at night during the past month—more than any other age group. And they reported being told by health care professionals that they have either depression or an anxiety disorder more than anyone else. One in five (19%) were told that they have depression or some kind of anxiety disorder—compared to 14% of those 34-47 years old, 12% of those 48-66, and 11% of those over 67. Among the top causes of this stress: job (or lack of job) related and "being stuck between debt and a dead-end," according to one of the Harris Interactive survey respondents.

There is no huge groundswell of support for Frederick Hayek and Ayn Rand, or T-shirts worshipping the totally free (but hugely damaged) spirit of Ozzy Osbourne, but a lot of the vision of hope and magic from 2008 is gone. Not simply on hold—gone. In 2012, there is a small but significant cadre of twenty –somethings adding luster to the movements of Congressman Ron Paul and Libertarian Party standard bearer Gary Johnson, a former governor of New Mexico. While Paul did not actually win any Republican primaries, he had the second highest number of delegates of any GOP hopeful. Johnson received much of his support among both Global Citizens and Nikes. The basis for that support? A nearly complete loss of confidence in not only government and politics, but also in a myriad of familiar institutions that no longer are seen as providers of security nor as problem-solvers.

For those of us who try to offer advice (both solicited and mainly unsolicited) to Globals, it is a hard sell to say "don't give up on the system and our leaders" or "you have a duty to vote." For whom? For what? At the same time, these kids are not seeing a Social Security or safety net check, not seeing any capacity to pay for security, are growing in resentment toward fifty-somethings for "staying on at jobs and refusing to give us a chance." They know that they and their children will foot the bill for national debt, but they don't have any clarity yet on how they are going to be able to afford that.

Globals do have a healthy respect for government and at the same time they have a libertarian sensibility regarding intrusions into their private lives. It is safe to say, they may vote Democrat to avoid the invasiveness of GOP positions on contraception and gay marriage amendments, and they clearly show very little inclination toward the GOP on anything else. Young people who want to get a fresh start in life are not looking for reductions in capital gains taxes or lifting moratoria on "hydrofracking" of natural gas. But they may be an essential ingredient in a major political party realignment that is inevitable.

I am often reminded of America's first "lost generation"—Dos Passos, Hemingway, Fitzgerald, Cummings, and others. Accomplished and successful, but they were indeed a jaded group and I cannot help but think about what might have been had they had a moment of financial success and a little piece of human happiness. I am worried about our First Globals. In 2008, I wrote so glowingly in *The Way We'll Be* about their potential and invested a lot of emotion into a group that I feel can lead us out of the current morass and malaise in which we find ourselves. They are not weighted down by outmoded bureaucracies, broken infrastructures, social relationships, or spatial limitations.

But I have seen such a sea change in them since the appearance of my 2008 book. Gone is the uber-confidence. ("Can you please tell me how I can become COO of Zogby International in a few years? I do have options."—to—"I am willing to do anything just to get started.") I talk differently to them (and to their parents, uncles, and aunts, who continue to call). But today they need help. Today. Right away.

The economy is missing them; management is missing them; the next great creative economy is being stalled in its formation because no candidate for president, neither political party, no church, no foundational societal institutions are sufficiently using this group's uncanny skills and energy. The good news is that of all age cohorts, the First Globals are the most sanguine about achieving the American Dream. While 55% of all adults say it is "possible for myself and my family to achieve the American Dream" and 29% say the American Dream "does not exist," 64% of Globals are positive and 23% are negative. They are the only cohort left where a majority believe that the middle class can achieve the American Dream. But the numbers were so much higher before the recession, and these young people are spending an extremely formative part of their lives with a more negative outlook than before.

Author Eric Liu, like the authors of this book, sees great things coming from our First Globals. In a *Time* magazine commentary entitled "Viewpoint: The Millennial Generation Can Lead Us Out of Gridlock," Liu is upbeat about how networked Globals "crowdfund charities, not go to fundraisers," how they are taking the lead in developing the "sharing economy" by pioneering companies like Airbnb and Car2Go, and how they are actually impacting local government with innovations like SeeClickFix, which alerts city hall about potholes. According to Liu, their vision is that "government should be big on the What and small on the How. ... [It should] set great national goals ... then use its platform and funding power to catalyze bottom-up and peer-to-peer solutions that can come from outside government."

Sounds like a very reasonable synthesis to us. Liu concludes with a potent warning to the two parties.

> If Democrats want to maintain their electoral hold on Millennials, they should start celebrating citizen-driven, non-governmental, networked ways to solve problems. And if Republicans hope to earn this generation's votes they should start acknowledging that there are indeed great national endeavors that require the leadership and spark of an active state. Whichever party disrupts its orthodoxy fastest can win the core of the 21st century electorate. By setting off this kind of race to reimagine, Millennials might just save American democracy.

With 72 million strong and perhaps even growing as those born in later years come of age, First Globals will re-shape our democracy.

# CHAPTER 7: GLOBALS AND INDEPENDENCE

Warning! What you are about to read was written by someone who is 64 years old. Mobility and outmoded concepts of space and geography are already having a huge impact on dating, marriage, and having children. Extensive polling and interviews reveal how "GlobalMobile" relationships will be developed and maintained, and how children will be raised. The good news is that the family does survive, but both terms of endearment and engagement are already being dramatically redefined. (One positive change may be the tossing out of overdone and outrageous destination weddings in Barcelona and Punta Cana.) Relationships and family are increasingly virtual, occasionally in-person, kid-in-tow, spatially challenged. Take comfort, mortgage and finance world, you were going down anyway before your venality did you in.

Nearly two in three First Globals (72%) do see marriage as part of their future, but one in four (24%) say that when they do marry, it is likely that they "may have to live apart from (their) spouse to meet financial responsibilities."

| "When you marry, how likely is it that you may have to live apart from your spouse to meet financial responsibilities?" ||||| 
|---|---|---|---|---|
|  | First Global | Nike | Woodstocker | Private |
| Likely | 24 | 11 | 4 | 0 |
| **Live in separate countries?** |||||
| Likely | 16 | 11 | 0 | 0 |
| **Share raising children in two different locations with a spouse or significant other?** |||||
| Likely | 15 | 11 | 28 | 0 |

We also want to address the social repercussions of delaying a young person's independence with the escalating number of children moving back in with their parents. Managing their lifestyle while launching their careers under their parents' roof can have a significant influence for an entire generation. They are taking longer to develop assets and studies link this to the tendency of putting off marriage and starting families. There could be a generational shift associated with the delay in family planning and attaining financial security.

One of the drivers that increases the number of Gen Yers who live with their parents post-graduation is the high cost of housing and living expenses. Rents escalated at a rapid pace as the housing market crashed and foreclosures flooded the market. The burden of a trillion dollars in student loans is compounded by having parents who are struggling to be able to afford retirement due to the economic downturn. The daunting budget required to manage housing costs, car payments, and student loans leads most of Gen Y toward either living with multiple roommates (a high-stress situation to many and a challenging environment in the early career-building stage) or to the alternative of living with mom and dad to save and get back on track. These costs are even higher for those who live in close proximity to large urban areas where many coveted jobs are located, but where the cost of living can be astronomical.

In addition to being forced to move back in with their parents because of the anemic job market and the high cost of housing, too many young people are encouraged to postpone graduation and hedge bets by changing their majors in college without regard for the high price tag attached to this life safari. With a lack of focus, students are taking longer to graduate as their search for the "right" major takes multiple detours. If students do not take the time to plan out their graduation requirements or seek counsel, they risk having to pay for additional semesters and delaying graduation.

And students who perform at a mediocre level in college will struggle even more in this tough economic climate. The competition for entry-level jobs is fierce, with top performers as well as current unemployed professionals with experience flooding the market. It is critical for students to take college seriously and to seek out opportunities to develop leadership and professional experience through internships. This trend will continue for as long as the job market continues to struggle.

If you don't want to be a part of these statistics, we issue the following advice to First Globals:

1. Get real hands-on experience as early as possible. Secure multiple internships; shadow alumni or professionals in your prospective industry of interest during the summer *and* during the school year to get a realistic perspective on what the job demands. Be ready to roll up your sleeves and do the work. To really understand the inner workings of being successful in any job, every industry requires heavy lifting up front. Demonstrate your commitment and work ethic by showing up early and always investing your best work into every project. It will pay off. Patience is key.

2. Develop professional presence to help you better represent yourself in interviews and when networking. Read up on the subject and aspire to executive comportment. The old sayings of "Dress two levels above the job you are interviewing for" and "Your first impression will either land you the job or the door" will hold true especially when you are interviewing with someone from the Gen X or Baby Boomer generation. Get a mentor, seek out alumni for insight and advice, use your college's career resources, and invest in your own professional development for free by doing some Internet research at the library.

3. Prioritize your financial savvy. Understand the financial implications of every decision. Balance your checkbook, build good credit and take a long-term approach with every

decision—academic, social, life. Debt will cripple you for far longer than you could even imagine while you living under your parents' roof.

4. Finally, sometimes you can do everything "right" and still be left with the only option of living at home with your parents. Don't let this be a setback. Let it be an opportunity to reset your goals and get ahead. Set a time limit for your stay and involve your parents in this goal. Commit to saving a certain percentage of your earnings (even if you are waiting tables while doing your job search) and put it away for your next step. If you can live without a car, use public transportation or coordinate with local peers in the same situation. Involving others with similar goals can accelerate motivation and achievement of the goal itself. Be respectful and grateful toward your parents for their support and live at home like a professional adult not as a repeat of your teenage self.

# CHAPTER 8: IMPACT OF FIRST GLOBAL WOMEN

While the themes we have discussed so far are inclusive of the entire generation, there are some important trends specific to First Global women that shed light on future workforce impact. "Having it all" has become an impossible quest for young women aiming to achieve high-level career success while raising a family, sustaining a healthy partnership, and maintaining size zero figures like every magazine-cover celebrity. Lately, young women have been inundated with media messages about the resurgence of domestic dominance through gourmet cooking and DIY home projects, adding to this pressure for perfection.

Lifetime's Women's Pulse Poll found that 85% of Gen Y women plan on remaining in the workforce after having children. This is one of the most difficult chapters for me (Joan) to write because I am in the midst of this process, as my husband and I anticipate the arrival of our first child and plan my re-entry into the workforce. I've always been extremely driven, which helped me pursue advanced degrees, fast track my corporate career, and grow my passions for leadership and mentoring. I recently launched a Lean In Circle (see more about Lean In and its founder Sheryl Sandberg below), presented my Fiscal 2014 budget and department strategy, celebrated at my baby shower, attended a fundraiser for the Girls Scouts of the USA hosted by Tea Leoni, and participated in a workshop aimed at developing women toward corporate board positions. My schedule has always been jam-packed, and I love living a full life. In the next couple months, enter baby. I know there will be change but where will it make the biggest impact? Despite everyone's finger wagging that I need to slow down, I haven't lost one ounce of my typical high energy and motivation. If anything, I feel more focused and driven than ever before to reach my goals so I can be a happy, healthy, and successful role model for my daughter.

Over the years, I have dived into the literature on career success and now on motherhood, babies, and dual roles, and that's why sharing my experience is important to me. Just like the women polled by Lifetime, I love seeing other women at the top of their fields and hope for a female president one day. But having worked in corporate life for 12 years, I know it's not easy for women to ascend to the highest levels—with or without children. A 2007 study conducted by Hudson,[1] a professional services firm, found that more than three-quarters of female middle managers aspire to senior-level executive positions. Yet, the statistics show that women are not making aggressive progress in secur-

---

1   Noonan, M., and S. McGowan. *The Ambition Divide: Differences Divide Women's Career Aspirations.* Hudson Thought Leadership Series, 4, 1. Available from: http://us.hudson.com/Portals/US/documents/White%20Papers/women-ambition-career-aspirations.pdf

ing these top spots. Organizations need to identify and provide support to women middle managers to retain and advance them. Too few companies, even those on the "Best Places for Women to Work" list, offer even minimal benefits for working moms or networks for women to come together and share best practices for career strategies. The women that I work with and mentor all state that their preference would be to stay with their current company but they are being forced to consider leaving for companies that have better benefits and more visible female leadership programs.

I encourage all First Global women to attend panels, workshops, and conferences, and read memoirs and books by women representing both sides of the mommy wars to get a strong perspective on the many decisions they will face if and when they become parents. Personally, it's thrilling to hear that so many more women want to make work + motherhood achievable because together we can change companies and career tracks to align with our needs in juggling both. (You know there is no balance, right? Every phase in life requires juggling.)

A recent paper by Connie Gersick, a Visiting Scholar at Yale School of Management, entitled "Having It All, Having Too Much, Having Too Little: How Women Manage Trade-Offs Through Adulthood"[2] looks at how some Baby Boomer women have answered the question "Can you have it all?" through their life experiences. The stories collected in the study are used to categorize the women and explore how each has handled trade-offs in her life. My experiences and approach are most aligned with the "Add and Delegate" category, as I strive for my ideal career, family, lifestyle and travel goals, while delegating activities along the way to make it happen. First Global women can reference studies like these for best practices on how to approach life decisions and deal with the setbacks that will present challenges to their lives and career goals.

My friend, Audrey McClelland, founder of Mom Generations, is a trailblazer for the new mom career track…the business of blogging. We met in 2005 at a weekend entrepreneurship incubator where Audrey and her mother had come to launch a full-time blog about motherhood and life that would help other women navigate products, companies, and topics, and make the best-informed decisions. Audrey had previously worked at Donna Karan in New York City before deciding to leave the corporate track to raise her four boys in Rhode Island with her husband. Seven years ago, with blogging and video testimonials still in their infancy, Audrey developed and promoted her content daily, sharing both her challenges and tender moments as a mom of four. Today, Mom Generations has more than 800 videos and 5,000 articles, 10,000 unique visits a day, and is a hip online destination for moms, featuring daily fashion news for moms and kids, fabulous giveaways, smart family advice, and the latest celebrity news. Audrey has been featured in ads by Proctor & Gamble, does product reviews for numerous household brand names, and has received sponsorships from global

---

[2] Gersick, C. (2013). *Having It All, Having Too Much, Having Too Little: How Women Manage Trade-Offs Through Adulthood.* Yale School of Management Working Paper. Available from: http://papers.ssrn.com/sol3/papers.cfm?abstract_id=2200581

companies like CVS Pharmacy, T. J. Maxx, and Kraft. She is also pregnant with her fifth child ... finally, a daughter!

Many women are following Audrey's lead by launching home-based businesses and abandoning the corporate track. Two motivations for this pivot are the need for more flexibility than they are able to find in their current workplace and a burning desire to express their creativity and other strengths that are not necessarily showcased in their current professional role. This path presents a few interesting questions: How will companies change to retain top performing family women rather than losing them to more flexible and creative entrepreneurial ventures? Can the home business career track be as profitable as the corporate track these women are leaving? And when will the stigma of the "mommy track" finally disappear from corporate America?

| "Two new books by prominent women are currently bestsellers. One is by Facebook executive Sheryl Sandberg called "Lean In: Women, Work and the Will to Lead" and maintains that women can have it all—family and career, as well the highest levels of leadership and management—but women have been reluctant to claim their own destiny. Sandberg says women have to want it all. The other is by prominent athlete and model Gabrielle Reece called "My Foot Is Too Big for the Glass Slipper: A Guide to the Less Than Perfect Life" who argues that women have a primary duty to family and are needed to first nurture and serve their families. Reece says that accepting a more traditional role is actually more a sign of strength for women. Which author comes closer to your view?" ||||
|---|---|---|---|---|
| | First Global | Nike | Woodstocker | Private |
| Sandberg/Reece—All | 39/27 | 25/35 | 25/35 | 16/32 |
| Sandberg/Reece—Women | 51/27 | 28/36 | 25/35 | 26/27 |
| Sandberg/Reece—Men | 27/29 | 22/34 | 26/37 | 4/36 |

A glance at the numbers above might suggest that the stronger agreement with Sandberg is a result of the life-cycle alone—i.e., young people want to dream of the future, they see big things happening in their lives and want to be a key force for change. But the level of support for "Lean In" among young women (51%) signifies a dramatic social change. Young women want both the highest level of achievement in their careers and in their families. Who will deny this majority of young women what they so earnestly want?

The media frenzy around this subject brings forth some boldly stated opinions. Glenn Beck recently weighed in on the media storm around women's roles at home and in the workplace: "Let me tell you something. You know who the strongest women are in the nation right now? The strongest women in the nation, more powerful, more self-confident than any other woman on the planet are the ones who stay home, the ones who raise their children, the ones who teach their children." His anti-Sandberg message targeted at young women implies that women who work full-time while raising their children are far from the ideal.

First Globals are less likely than any other age cohort to agree with Beck on this issue.

First Global women are re-creating the image of the "successful career woman." She can wear power suits and speak up while providing authentic inspiration to her teams. The new career girl should follow Sandberg's lead and leave work early to attend her child's kindergarten graduation, launch a side hustle (i.e., entrepreneurial venture), and serve on a community board even while working for a traditional organization. Having experienced the impact of the Enron debacle, 9/11, the downturn in the real estate market, and a tanking economy, First Global women are adapting their skills to take charge of their own fate. The frequently cited statistics surrounding the gaps in pay between women and their male colleagues should motivate this generation to negotiate and ask for their worth. There are so many great resources targeted directly to women such as DailyWorth, LearnVest, Citi's Women & Co., and the Little PINK Book that offer tips, advice, and tools. Another great resource is Linda Babcock's book *Ask for It* (Bantam, 2009) and her training program at the Heinz College Negotiation Academy for Women.

If First Global women make the effort to evaluate the environment that best fits their personal needs and preferences, they will become clear about what is needed at work to help them stay successful and advance. Building a network of women and men who support their potential can help them grow stronger in their confidence to demand the changes in the workplace or make the move to seek out organizations that best align with their values.

# PART II

# Management Strategies and Solutions to Unleash the Potential of First Globals

We have spent the previous eight chapters describing the unique and compelling characteristics of the First Global generation, supporting our message of their value to every organization and to the U.S. economy. Many times we have offered our advice and opinions for unleashing their potential but the following chapters provide global management strategies and big idea solutions that will help you as a leader, an organization, a mentor, or an advocate to drive large-scale change. We hope you will use this as a blueprint for unleashing the potential of the First Global Generation.

# CHAPTER 9: HARNESSING THE TALENT AND EFFECTIVE MANAGEMENT STRATEGIES

### For Senior Leaders

The glove does not seem to fit. In 2011, the Conference Board conducted a global survey of more than 500 CEOs which revealed that talent-related issues are among the greatest concerns for top business leaders. Across the board, all the countries who responded ranked 'talent'—"finding it, growing it, keeping it, and rewarding it"—as one their top five CEO challenges.

At the same time, our youngest adults are currently experiencing one of the highest levels of unemployment in history. One in eleven college graduates are leaving school without a job, often averaging around six months of unemployment before landing their first job. Here is the strange disconnect. In an economy with an overflowing number of highly educated young adults eager to enter the working world, companies are expressing their concern about finding talent and retaining it. With such a huge pool of candidates to choose from, are these graduates simply not "talented" enough for these companies? And why are so many of the talented Millennials that do wind up in these large companies leaving after only a year or two?

Joan has been branded The Millennial Matchmaker™, connecting the talent in the Millennial generation to organizations and advocating for increased investment in these relationships so that Millennials stick around for the long haul. Here is a preview of her message to organizations who want to attract and retain young talent:

> The way in which companies are defining "talent" is inconsistent with the assets the Millennial generation bring to the table. Hence, companies will continue to suffer from "talent block" until they recognize that Millennials possess an entirely different, but just as valuable, set of essential skills. Once this fact is accepted and an environment is created to foster this talent, Millennials and corporate America will be able to mutually promote each other's growth and success.

### For Managers

**Dismissive Management: Lack of advancement, encouragement and support**

- Management issues: If an organization, particularly its management team, has a dismissive attitude or lacks the ability to connect with younger employees (First Globals and even Generation X), then they are likely to face a costly turnover. The loss of constructive communication eliminates valuable expertise transfer about the organization that is essential to future success and sustainability. Poor relationships between managers and First Globals prevent the necessary sharing and exchange needed. Mutually respectful relationships, which start with an understanding of one another's values and differing strengths, are critical.

- Advancement: Let Millennials know that they can advance, and establish programs that will support accelerated development. Allow high achievers who show the potential to rise up the ranks quickly to do so. Challenge them with global assignments and cross-functional project management that exposes them to all areas and strategies in the business. For this generation, advancement is more about accelerated growth than ego and power.

### For First Globals

Here's some advice for First Globals as you plan your career strategies and set off to achieve your goals:

Obviously, do not give up. Your drive, ambition, and commitment to making a difference will keep you on the right track. Schedule time with yourself at least once a week to review your professional and personal goals in case you need to pivot your focus in a different direction or pat yourself on the back for your progress.

Relationships are everything. It's more than just networking with business cards, you have to make an effort to get to know others who are in roles that interest you or are the type of leader you aspire to be. Do your research before you contact them for a coffee or an informational meeting. Show genuine interest in hearing their stories and about the work they do. Don't make it all about you. If you build an authentic relationship with a mentor or potential hiring manager up front, there will be natural opportunities for you to share your strengths and goals.

Finding and keeping talent is a top priority for every leader in every sector. Continue to invest in self-development after you graduate through online programs, research, and attendance at conferences or live workshops to sharpen and expand your skills and stay "in the know" for your field.

Be focused when sharing your goals. Recent graduates often write to me sharing their "dream to work in New York" and asking "Can you help me find a great company?" My reaction to such entreaties is simply: "Ugh!" I am not interested in being anyone's pocket guide to New York living, nor am I impressed by someone who seeks to shift all the responsibility for their job search onto me. The Globals who stand out (and to whom I am willing to hand over my Rolodex!) are those who:

- Research the field they are interested in and align their professional activities and work experiences with it.

- Have clean social media profiles (Linked In, Facebook, Twitter, etc.) that present them in a positive manner. Companies review these sites before making decisions about interviewing and hiring. Employees are an extension of their company's brand, and companies want to ensure that their employees reflect their values and exhibit professionalism. Your resume must also be updated and focused.

The following advice is specifically for those First Globals who are managing and leading others with more experience and tenure:

1. Show respect up front for the experience, tenure, and contributions of those around you. Make it clear that you value their perspective and history with the company and in their field.

2. Just as you seek respect and understanding for your style of approaching work, make an effort to understand others' preferred work style, communication preferences, work environment, and approach to professional relationships. Initiate these conversations and make time to share your perspectives in an effort to build trust. Discuss expectations including what they would like from you as their supervisor and what you would like from them.

3. Don't be afraid to:

    - Explore their goals. Don't assume that they do not have aspirations for more responsibility because of their age and current position. Ask what they want out of this role, about their daily experience and structure of responsibilities, what areas of development they would appreciate (e.g., courses, trainings, cross-functional project exposure). The point is talk to them, get to know them, and explore their motivators and preferred style of recognition.

    - Use them as a sounding board. Show them that you value their opinion and perspective by involving them in strategic decisions or brainstorming. Be inclusive of all of your team members' contributions. Today's successful leadership model is more about collaboration than dictatorial management.

4. Learn all you can from generations before you. Learn about processes and protocols that have worked or failed in the past. Listen to "war stories" and the lessons others have learned in

current and previous roles. Learn about the evolution of your industry and business—how the environment and "way of doing things" at this company or elsewhere has changed over time and how they feel about it. Listening goes a LONG way. Ask about their personal experiences with this company, customers, and colleagues to gain insights, as well as to learn about your matrix partners through their eyes. This may also provide you with a heads-up about where they may have some bias or influence.

It will be challenging at times to build relationships and trust across generations so keep in mind that the keys are open communication and respect. Determine a set time on a regular basis for check-ins and DO NOT miss them, reschedule them a million times, or disregard the impact these regular discussions will have on the senior professional's work ethic, loyalty to you, and your team's goals and engagement. Don't be intimidated because at the end of day if you demonstrate the qualities of an authentic leader—if you prioritize your people, show you care and they matter to you, truly listen and value their ideas, respect their experience and contributions, and foster a positive atmosphere—they will respect you and appreciate working for someone like you. I've led individuals that had higher-ranking positions than my own in their past and learned that I could never accomplish the magnitude of our goals and impact without them. I treat them as partners but still provide direction, and honest and timely feedback.

# CHAPTER 10: SCALABLE GLOBAL TRAINING AND ENGAGEMENT SOLUTIONS TO THE JOBS CRISIS AND THE TALENT GAP

An important gap in bringing First Globals into today's workplace is the development and delivery of scalable training models that will help them truly succeed. This need applies to young people who are headed in every direction—the private sector, every professional service from law firms to engineering companies, non-profits, start-up businesses and entrepreneurial venture environments, and even the military. Long-term success begins with the very first experiences that First Globals have in their new places of work and the manner in which expectations are set.

We would like to share two unique models that aim to support young people in this transitional period, *The Fullbridge Program* and *The Millennial Train* as well as a more common corporate leadership development example. We follow these profiles with our recommended strategy for rethinking your approach to training and engagement to help you better align with First Global learning preferences and the prioritization of this generation as a critical workforce. No matter how large or small the organization, the diversity of mission or ultimate product or service, the investment you make in the First Global workforce will have a tremendous impact on their loyalty, their productivity, and your future success.

In Chapter 2, we mentioned The Fullbridge Program, which was built around a mission of preparing young people for their first foray into the workplace so that they're on a path not only to success, but also to satisfaction. Luke Owings, a millennial who plays a key leadership role in the organization, shared his passion for creating an environment where young people can prepare themselves and more experienced people can garner value from sharing what they know and who they are.

Luke also shared that the Fullbridge Program approaches training as…

> …a way that actually requires them [First Globals] to do things which is a way to get beyond all of the issues of perceived coddling and giving them special attention. You're

not talking about doing things. You're doing things. Work doesn't happen alone. You're working with a broad group of people of different capabilities and skills. Mentors are focused on guiding participants through the learning more than information sharing. This involves orienting, setting expectations, giving feedback, and being devoted to development. It begins with plenty of scaffolding to support participants in their learning, but gradually removes them in a way that challenges them to continue to learn and grow. Situations are diverse enough that participants must play different roles in different situations.

The Fullbridge Program stresses exercise-based learning experiences that also have the benefits of an apprenticeship. The curriculum for the program covers the basic skill categories needed to approach real-life business challenges in traditional or entrepreneurial environments. The involvement of mentors and the emphasis on dynamic facilitation by the core instructors set this program apart from the typical leadership development programs offered solely by either educational institutions or corporations themselves. To counter the tendency of First Globals' not asking for help, the Fullbridge coaches openly address the requirement for speaking up.

> As time goes on, they put more and more of the onus on the proactivity of the participants. They do this by being in the room less and less, as well as setting up shop down the hallway. All of this is designed so that participants learn how to ask their boss for help. This whole situation is also designed to make their peers the path of least resistance for help. This is an extremely crucial skill in today's world as they need to learn how to work together not just when it's been mandated from above.

The success of Fullbridge has spawned growth opportunities around the world; it has the ability to customize tracks for specific fields like law and the military as well as to be integrated into higher education itself.

Taking training on the road, literally, is the core design of The Millennial Trains Project (MTP). MTP is a 10-day train journey from San Francisco to Washington, D.C., with 100 enterprising Millennials on board. Using crowd-funded interventions to support the big ideas of the Millennials who are selected for the transcontinental journey, the program is designed to provide opportunities at each stop for the participants to engage with their peers around their project and attend workshops with local leaders and mentors, while exploring America's new frontiers.

The MTP mission "is to enable passengers and virtual audiences to identify, evaluate, and explore emerging opportunities and challenges in communities where our trains stop while advancing a project that benefits, serves, and inspires others." The idea was inspired by a similar program that the founder participated in based in India which drew 20,000 Millennials' applications last year competing for 400 spots. Patrick Dowd, MTP founder, shares his philosophy that "journeys build leaders" and that "tapping back into this idea of the pioneering spirit that built our country" by using trains with an emphasis on action, connection to landscape, and contributing to the welfare of the country make it unique.

It has become more common over the last decade for larger organizations to offer development and management training programs for young leaders especially in the accounting, finance, consulting, and health care industries. A unique program launched by Deloitte focuses on providing global experiences for internships. According to Deloitte's website:

> Global Interns will be chosen … from a select group of incoming interns from countries around the world. If you are selected for the GIP, you'll spend approximately four weeks in a host country where you will learn about business issues from a new and different perspective, work in a team to address real business challenges, develop your cross-cultural awareness, and build a first-class, truly global network. The result? An enriching and dynamic experience, and the knowledge and experience you will gain will enhance your career—wherever it may take you.

This approach aligns with the values of First Globals to live and work outside their home country and to be exposed to different cultures and business practices. It's a smart recruiting tool for Deloitte.

# CHAPTER 11: A PRESIDENTIAL SUMMIT BETWEEN CORPORATE AND WALL STREET LEADERS ...

As a nation, we need to ask some key questions: How much is it worth to us to develop America's highly talented next workforce? Can we stay competitive and innovative if we cannot place and train the next generation of Americans in career path experiences? What happens to us (the planet, let alone the United States) and to First Globals, if we waste another few years letting them languish? This issue is Cabinet-level, C-Suite level—for government, corporate, and non-governmental leadership. It also requires that First Globals be present at the table when their (and our) future is at stake.

We need to extract promises from these leaders for actual amounts of money to be invested. The alternative? They watch their money stagnate and both the economy and human capital weaken. We closely watch developing nations with huge numbers of people under 30, and we are smart enough to see dollar signs and investment opportunities in these burgeoning consumer markets. American corporations and agencies like the Agency for International Development have programs that focus on nurturing skills in Africa, Latin America, and the Middle East. But the United States presently has tens of millions of educated young people—numbers that are larger than most developing nations—that are in many ways "all dressed up with nowhere to go."

Fostering entrepreneurship (both private and social), providing opportunities to connect and broaden their networks with young people worldwide who share similar interests and need training, fostering opportunities to meet social needs with creative new "apps," and providing start-up capital for new ventures and gigs—all of these are things that need immediate attention and, just as importantly, a central focus and clearinghouse.

Representatives from venture capital, higher education (from top private and public universities as well as community colleges), and entrepreneurs must be present. As for the Wall Streeters, let's call this just what it is: a combination of an exercise in community service and an investment in an "emerging market" of 70 million people.

# CHAPTER 12:
# ... AND THE CREATION OF AMERICA'S FIRST GLOBALS CITIZENS FUND

One way to demonstrate a commitment is to contribute a substantial amount of resources. The United States needs a huge fund created that will be managed by private equity and NGO professionals. Here is the reality: There is plenty of capital, approximately $2 trillion in private cash that is just sitting there. And there are CENGAs who need to get started, who need to develop and hone their entrepreneurial skills to survive and thrive in the gig economy. There is plenty of need and plenty of money. Securing investment capital is not the only story. The fund needs to ensure proper funding, oversight, and mentoring for entrepreneurial development. One way to both get the most talented people and set the stage for the future is to "commission" Wall Street rule-breakers to do their "community service" by administering such a fund, and training and helping to hone the skills of talented and under-employed First Globals to become NextGen administrators. (This might also serve to push the Justice Department to prosecute more violators.)

At the elegant campus of SUNY Fredonia, south of Buffalo, there is an entrepreneurial class. A team of students, responding to an unfortunate rash of teen suicides, set up an app that provided counseling and a link to a friendly voice for teenagers in crisis. This kind of social entrepreneurship actually makes money while meeting a pressing need. But who will provide the microloan to make sure that the service continues, expands, and reaches the teens who need it?

Speaking of microloans. They always work best when overseen by a committee of peers—i.e. fellow loan recipients. In Africa and Asia, microloans are awarded and governed by village committees. Let First Global Citizens review proposals for new business and technical training loans. Good proposals that will allow young people to become business, social capital, or independent contractors can be reviewed, awarded, and tweaked by this large social network. Awards can be small to mid-sized, in the form of cash or extensions on student loans. Paybacks can be made in cash or forgiveness on student loans.

There is mutual experience and understanding, as well as the necessary peer pressure to make them work. If structured around peer review and decision-making, this fund also can breed a self-sustaining program. It provides good experience for both recipients and reviewers.

And at a time when, as noted in Part I, young Americans lack confidence in government and corporations, a commitment like this can go a long way toward helping to restore (or even create for the first time) some faith in these societal pillars.

All of this done by private equity and generated by presidential leadership. Add to that full support from both the Democrats and GOP because we all pledge allegiance to private equity. Besides, the stakes are too high. We need to all address our CENGA problem to prevent it from a becoming a longer term crisis.

The First Global Citizens Fund should itself be entrepreneurial: low-interest loans, revolving and regenerating. Through wise investments in America's largest emerging market, it can actually make decent money for its investors.

# CHAPTER 13: FIRST GLOBALS TECHNOLOGY CORPS

I (John) spent some time in North Africa in the autumn of 2011 and the spring of 2012 and was struck by the consistency of themes coming from opposite directions, but never quite connecting. My polling and focus groups among young supporters of the Arab Spring in Tunisia revealed their strong desire to become leaders in the New Tunisia. These were the first young people to defy an Arab dictator and peacefully drive him from office. But now, young Tunisians both in the country and in the diaspora, want the fruit of their hard work. They want to serve in government, lead NGO efforts to build democracy and economic capacity, and modernize their economy. They want the best 21st century skills, and their mantra is "technical support and training." They told this to any and every American or European official (and pollster) they saw.

It was a powerful reminder of a similar message I received from a poll of the Emirates-based Young Arab Leaders, which I conducted in August 2006 for Business for Diplomatic Action. Back then, my company surveyed more than 200 members of this network of Arabs under 45 years of age—men and women, business and professional, on the make, mainly located in the Gulf region but also scattered across the Middle East and North Africa. Aside from family, we asked what was most important to them. Success in their profession and business was by far the top answer. What did they need to attain that success? They were clear: the best possible training, mentoring, internships, and hands-on work opportunities. And, from a list of developed countries presented, where would they expect to get the best skill development? The response wasn't even close—it was the United States, "the platinum standard," according to one survey respondent. But then we asked who their number one hero in the Arab World was. There was a consensus: Hassan Nasrallah, the leader of Hezbollah, because he had just "stood up to the United States." What a disconnect—and yet what a clear opportunity for the United States in so many ways.

On one hand, we have a burgeoning leadership class in this huge region crying out for technical support and training. On the other hand, the United States has an army of twenty-somethings with the best available education, desirous to be mobile, passionate about changing the world, and unable to find decent enough jobs. While the U.S. Department of State is fond of funding $100 million grants that employ overpriced consultants and private security forces, why not take a page from

President John F. Kennedy's Peace Corps and hire America's First Globals at a much more reasonable stipend and place them in a situation where they meet and learn together from their fellow Globals, provide technical support, and build a bridge with another culture? This could and should move well beyond the Arab and Muslim worlds. I have raised this with the highest levels of the State Department and they are "pursuing it," which I actually believe. What an excellent way to address a number of issues altogether and for a much more affordable rate.

# CONCLUSION

So much of the literature written and blogosphere discussion about Millennials has been about their self-centered-ness, even outright selfishness, immaturity, deferred adulthood, and laziness. To a great degree this is simply ahistorical and out of context. For nearly one hundred years (think the "Roaring Twenties" era of flappers, fraternity pranks, bathtub gin, automobiles denounced as "houses of prostitution on wheels"), twenty-somethings have been generally focused on themselves. "Hooking up," staying at home until married, low-end start-up jobs (especially for young women) are not really new at all. Over the past three decades, parents have structured the lives of First Globals and raised their (and our) expectations too much, just as we have (until 2007 at least) proffered too many choices that were bound to be unfulfilled. With so many going to college and accumulating so much student loan debt, it is not surprising at all that there is a lot of impatience, disillusionment, and deferred (even lost) dreams.

Our book is a revisionist examination of who First Globals really are, what they have to offer, and how they are the best equipped of all to thrive and solve the problems of our shared world today and tomorrow. It is a call to action, a handbook for those who lead and want to lead, and a more holistic depiction of an outstanding group with so much potential.

It doesn't do any good to bash an entire age cohort. They are destined by their sheer numbers and outstanding talents to lead the world. Let's get busy.

## CONTACT THE AUTHORS:

**John Zogby,** founder of the "Zogby Poll" and the Zogby companies, is an internationally respected pollster, opinion leader, and best-selling author. He has joined with his son Jonathan Zogby as Senior Analyst. A much sought-after speaker, he is represented by the American Program Bureau of Boston.

"All hail Zogby, the maverick predictor," decreed The Washington Post, when John Zogby called the 1996 presidential election with pinpoint accuracy. And he did it again in the following two elections. His presidential polling remains among the most accurate through five elections. He has served as an on-air election analyst for NBC News, BBC, CBC, ABC (Australia), and has been featured by the Foreign Press Center in Washington every election night since 1998.

With the Zogby Poll, the "second best known polling brand in the US today" (Washington Post), John Zogby remains the hottest and most accurate pollster and analyst of America's political and cultural landscape. In addition to the global reach of his brand, Zogby Polls have been cited frequently in popular culture, including NBC's *West Wing,* CW's *Gossip Girls,* Netflix series *House of Cards,* and numerous novels, game shows, and the 25th Anniversary edition of Trivial Pursuit. Zogby Polls are regularly cited on *The Tonight Show* and spoofed on The Late Show and NPR's *All Things Considered. Fortune Magazine, The New Yorker* and *Investor's Business Daily* have all profiled John Zogby. He has appeared on every major U.S. television network, the BBC and scores of U.S. broadcasts. His appearances on *The Daily Show with Jon Stewart* are among his favorites.

Called "The Prince of Polling" by political strategist Mary Matalin, John Zogby's interactive methodology is a leader in the industry. He is the author of the best-selling *The Way We'll Be: The Zogby Report on the Transformation of the American Dream* (Random House, 2008).

Zogby writes weekly columns on *Forbes.com* and contributes a weekly Obama report card to *The Washington Examiner's* Washington Secrets, by Paul Bedard. He is also a founding contributor to The Huffington Post. His analytical expertise has also been published on the opinion pages of the *New York Times, Wall Street Journal* and *Financial Times.*

He has polled and consulted for a wide spectrum of business, media, government, and political groups including Coca-Cola, Microsoft, CISCO Systems, St. Jude's Children's Research Hospital, and the U.S. Census Bureau.

A well-known political and social pundit, his work has been featured in op-ed pages worldwide, valued in corporate boardrooms, and considered "must-read" at every level of America's political landscape.

A senior advisor at the Kennedy School of Government at Harvard University, Zogby also serves as a Commissioner for the Center for Strategic and International Studies (CSIS) Commission on Smart Power and is a senior fellow of the Catholic University Institute for Policy Research and Catholic Studies. As Chairman of Sudan Sunrise, Zogby works to continue the vision of NBA player Manute Bol to bring peace to Sudan through education. He is presently chairman of the capital campaign on behalf of Mohawk Valley Community College (where he taught in the 1970s), and serves on the boards of the Arab American Institute, Upstate Venture Connect (which links young entrepreneurs with venture capital in Upstate New York), and Freedom Guide Dogs for the Blind and Visually Impaired.

Zogby has been awarded three honorary doctorates from the State University of New York, the College of St. Rose, and the Graduate School of Union University. In 2008, he was awarded the Chancellor's Distinguished Fellows Award from the University of California Irvine.

John can be reached at john@zogbyanalytics.com. Visit the company website at www.zogbyanalytics.com. For speaking engagements, contact the American Program Bureau at www.apbspeakers.com. Follow John on twitter @thejohnzogby and feel free to send ideas to promote the discussion.

After a decade of mentoring and leading thousands of Millennials from around the world to help them achieve their potential, **Joan Snyder Kuhl** launched Why Millennials Matter, a Gen-Y speaking and consulting company based in New York City. Why Millennials Matter is focused on raising awareness among employers about the value of investing in their future workforce. Organizations are struggling to attract and retain Millennials (Generation Y) because they lack the insights into what this generation wants out of their employer and the benefits that will inspire their loyalty. The same struggle exists for organizations that are trying to connect with the Millennial consumer through marketing and product development.

As a keynote speaker, Joan delivers engaging presentations that incorporate the latest research and insights around generational dynamics in the workplace and her personal experiences hiring, developing, coaching and managing Millennials. As a sought after keynoter and panelist for conferences, Joan helps inspire students, new grads, parents, and professionals. Joan's coaching and leadership trainings have impacted diverse audiences of Millennials across the United States and as far away as Dubai, China, Ghana, Australia, and India.

Joan has a long and active commitment to empowering young leaders to achieve their potential as a mentor and coach. Since 2005, Joan has spoken to thousands of high school and college students as a trained speaker for the Making It Count Program on Career and College preparation for success. Joan serves as the youngest board member for the Frances Hesselbein Leadership Institute named after the former CEO of the Girls Scouts of the USA and recipient of the Presidential Medal of

Freedom. More than 525 leaders from 37 countries representing 375+ organizations joined a global webinar to hear Joan and Frances Hesselbein on "Women in the Lead" on March 9, 2011. Joan is frequently invited to speak to undergraduate and MBA students including Babson, Wellesley, Olin College of Engineering, NYU, University of Pittsburgh, Rutgers University, and LIM College.

While pursuing a career in the fields of business and health care, Joan has used her background of leadership in both the private and social sectors. Joan has more than 12 years of corporate management experience working at a Fortune 500 company in the roles of sales, marketing, organizational effectiveness, training and development. She has been recognized for her turnaround tactics leading teams to high performance results and developing corporate wide training initiatives.

The experience of coaching and mentoring Gen Y'ers about workforce issues—and being responsible for managing and developing them in a corporate environment— gives Joan a unique perspective. Finding commonalities amongst all four generations in the workplace is a key component to engage Generation Y's employee loyalty and performance.

Joan works with clients to become Millennial Ready by assessing and developing programs, branding initiatives and management training to attract, retain and promote young talent. The results for the organization are to be seen as the Preferred Employer to Millennials and as an organization that is on the pulse of the Millennial customer needs.

While serving as Student Government President at the University of Pittsburgh, Joan began honing her leadership skills. She was the student speaker at her own undergraduate graduation and invited back as an alumni commencement speaker. She earned an MBA from Rutgers University and studied global business strategies in Beijing and Shanghai, China. In 2011, Joan became certified in the Principles and Practices of Organizational Development through the Executive Change and Consultation program at Columbia University in New York, NY.

Follow Joan on Twitter: @joansnyderkuhl. Visit her website at http://www.joanksnyder.com. For speaking and media inquiries, contact: joan@joanksnyder.com.

# APPENDIX: FIRST GLOBALS DEMOGRAPHICS (%)

|  | FIRST GLOBALS |
|---|---|
| Men | 50.5 |
| Women | 49.5 |
| Less than $25,000 | 27 |
| $25,000-$50,000 | 35 |
| $50,000-$75,000 | 15 |
| $75,000-$100,000 | 8 |
| $100,000-$150,000 | 9 |
| $150,000+ | 7 |

|  | FIRST GLOBALS | NIKES | WOODSTOCKERS | PRIVATES |
|---|---|---|---|---|
| Big City | 25 | 28 | 25 | 25 |
| Small City | 24 | 17 | 19 | 17 |
| Suburb | 33 | 39 | 35 | 36 |
| Rural | 18 | 16 | 21 | 19 |
| Married | 31 | 67 | 60 | 53 |
| NASCAR Fan | 26 | 31 | 23 | 31 |
| Current Job is Career | 40 | 51 | 32 | 14 |
| Current Job is Gig | 29 | 24 | 21 | 9 |
| Social Networker | 58 | 47 | 25 | 19 |
| Weekly Wal-Mart | 33 | 31 | 24 | 18 |
| Creative Job Sector | 30 | 21 | 21 | 12 |
| Creative Class ID | 33 | 30 | 36 | 28 |
| White | 55 | 65 | 78 | 79 |
| Hispanic | 22 | 17 | 7 | 2 |
| African American | 13 | 9 | 11 | 18 |
| Asian | 9 | 6 | 1 | - |
| Democrat | 43 | 38 | 31 | 46 |
| Republican | 25 | 28 | 43 | 34 |
| Independent | 31 | 35 | 27 | 20 |
| Liberal | 34 | 26 | 24 | 18 |
| Moderate | 34 | 37 | 28 | 35 |
| Conservative | 32 | 38 | 48 | 47 |
| Tea Party | 17 | 24 | 26 | 32 |
| Occupy Wall Street | 19 | 22 | 15 | 15 |